Speaking Like Magpies

Frank McGuinness was born in Buncrana, Co. Donegal, and now lives in Dublin and lectures in English at University College Dublin. His plays include: *The Factory Girls* (Abbey Theatre, Dublin, 1982), *Baglady* (Abbey, 1985), *Observe the Sons of Ulster Marching Towards the Somme* (Abbey, 1985; Hampstead Theatre, London, 1986), *Innocence* (Gate Theatre, Dublin, 1986), *Carthaginians* (Abbey, 1988; Hampstead, 1989), *Mary and Lizzie* (RSC, 1989), *The Bread Man* (Gate, 1991), *Someone Who'll Watch Over Me* (Hampstead, West End and Broadway, 1992), *The Bird Sanctuary* (Abbey, 1994), *Mutabilitie* (NT, 1997), *Dolly West's Kitchen* (Abbey, 1999; Old Vic, 2000) and *Gates of Gold* (Gate, 2002). His translations include Ibsen's *Rosmersholm* (NT, 1987), *Peer Gynt* (Gate, 1988; RSC and international tour, 1994; NT, 2000), Chekhov's *Three Sisters* (Gate and Royal Court, 1990), Lorca's *Yerma* (Abbey, 1987), Brecht's *The Threepenny Opera* (Gate, 1991), *Hedda Gabler* (Roundabout Theatre, Broadway, 1994), *Uncle Vanya* (Field Day production, 1995), *A Doll's House* (Playhouse Theatre, Broadway, 1997), *The Caucasian Chalk Circle* (NT, 1997), Sophocles' *Electra* (Donmar, Broadway, 1998), Ostrovsky's *The Storm* (Almeida, 1998), *The Wild Duck* (Abbey, 2003) and Euripides' *Hecuba* (Donmar, 2004).

FRANK McGUINNESS

Speaking Like Magpies

faber and faber

First published in 2005
by Faber and Faber Limited
3 Queen Square, London WCIN 3AU

Typeset by Country Setting, Kingsdown, Kent CT14 8ES
Printed in England by Mackays of Chatham plc, Chatham, Kent

A CIP record for this book
is available from the British Library

0-571-23081-4

2 4 6 8 10 9 7 5 3 1

Speaking Like Magpies was first performed by the Royal Shakespeare Company at the Swan Theatre, Stratford-upon-Avon, on 21 September 2005. The cast in order of appearance was as follows:

The Equivocator Kevin Harvey
Mary Queen of Scots Michelle Butterly
King James William Houston
Queen Anne Teresa Banham
Two Ladies-in-Waiting Michelle Butterly,
    Miranda Colchester
Gentlemen Barry Aird, Jon Foster, Keith Osborn
A Puritan Keith Osborn
A Pope Julian Stolzenberg
Two Dogs Peter Bramhill, Jon Foster
Henry Garnet Fred Ridgeway
May Vinette Robinson
Robert Cecil Nigel Cooke
Lady Anne Vaux Ishia Bennison
Robert Catesby Jonjo O'Neill
Robin Wintour Matt Ryan
Guy Fawkes Barry Aird
A Catholic Aristocrat Keith Osborn
A Protestant Divine Jon Foster
Conspirators Peter Bramhill, Jon Foster, Keith Osborn,
    Julian Stolzenberg

All other parts played by members of the company.

Directed by Rupert Goold
Designed by Matthew Wright
Lighting designed by Wayne Dowdeswell
Music and sound score by Adam Cork
Movement by Michael Ashcroft
Fights by Terry King
Assistant Director Elizabeth Freestone
Company voice work by Jeannette Nelson
Costume Supervisor Poppy Hall
Production Manager Simon Ash
Stage Manager Zoë Donegan

Characters

The Equivocator
Mary Queen of Scots
Elizabeth I
King James
Queen Anne
Ladies-in-Waiting
Gentlemen
A Puritan
A Pope
Two Dogs
Henry Garnet
May
Robert Cecil
Lady Anne Vaux
Robert Catesby
Robin Wintour
Guy Fawkes
A Catholic Aristocrat
A Protestant Divine
Conspirators

FOR JACKIE HILL

ONE: THE TWO QUEENS

In a pool of light the Equivocator stands.

He will be seen by some characters in the play. For each of these characters he will perform a different function.

To others he is unseen and unheard, unless he so chooses.

Although he is entirely human in form he resembles the satyr in Piero di Cosimo's painting Satyr Weeping Over A Nymph (*National Gallery, London*).

EQUIVOCATOR

I am the equivocator.
What I say I mean.
I ask you to believe me.
Give me your faith.
In return I give you –
What will I give?

A story you know the end of.
The king is not killed.
The plotters get caught.
There is no big bang.
Remember, remember –
How do we remember?

May I help you?
May this be my gift?
May I take you to worlds
You could not remember?

No harm is promised.
Security is assured.

No risk to life or limb.
Nothing shall explode.
Give me your faith.

A woman lay dying,
Her last days as queen,
We expect her here,
Not in hell,
Not in heaven,
Not on the earth –
But where souls gather
At the point of death.

A burst of light.
   An open coffin appears. It contains the body of
Elizabeth I.
   There is soft music.

EQUIVOCATOR

This is her body,
Elizabeth of her realm,
Beloved virgin,
We waited for you,
To greet you, dead,
To receive your spirit,
To anoint her majesty
With cold chrism.
She who ruled England –
Great Gloriana.

Welcome to this world –
Your name is nothing.
Your power is nothing.
You own nothing.
You've turned to nothing.
Can you hear me?
Have you become deaf as stone?
Give me your faith.

In return I give you –
What will I give?
A spirit, a sound,
A sight for sore eyes,
Someone you know.
She has been waiting,
Waiting to receive you,
Waiting for years.
She will speak
Into your dead ears.
You will touch her
With your icy hands,
You will smell
The scent of the dead,
You will taste
The dead's tasteless kiss,
Breathe their breathless breath,
She is your cousin,
The queen of Scots.

In a gentle light, Mary Queen of Scots appears.
    She is dressed magnificently in gold and black.
    *She has been restored to a young woman, in stark
contrast to dead Elizabeth.*
    Mary carries a small silver vessel, containing holy oil.

MARY

Sweet cousin, sleep.
Dream in your coffin.
I have saved you from hell.

I forgive your crimes –
See, how I forgive.
As you were anointed queen,
I will anoint you anew,
I will cleanse your five senses,
Purge your body's sins.

3

Sleep, sweet cousin.

There is music as Mary makes the Sign of the Cross on Elizabeth's feet with the holy oil.

Your feet that danced
Before false prophets,
They are each forgiven.

Mary repeats the gesture on Elizabeth's hands.

Your hands that raised
The looking glass
To marvel at your beauty,
They are each forgiven.

Mary repeats the gesture on Elizabeth's eyes.

Your eyes that blazed
And burned to ash
Any who offended,
They are each forgiven.

Mary repeats the gesture on Elizabeth's lips.

Your tongue, your lips
That spoke the sin
To send me to the sword,
They are each forgiven.

Mary anoints Elizabeth's ears and nose with oil.

Your ears that heard,
Your nose that smelt
All secrets against you,
They are each forgiven.
This is my gift.
And in return I ask –
What do I ask for?
What I have been given.
My son succeeds you.

My James, my boy, my vengeance.
For this I forgive you.
I have saved you from hell.

EQUIVOCATOR
How have you that power?

MARY
I was given it.

EQUIVOCATOR
Tell us – who by – tell us.

MARY
A king of my acquaintance.

EQUIVOCATOR
A lover –
God loves Mary Queen of Scots?

MARY
No, he loves my son.
He loves my James.
He gives him the world.

EQUIVOCATOR
The throne of England –

MARY
Ample. It is ample.
Ask her – she died defending it.
A maid – a stinking one
That I must now embrace.
Time for her to waken.

EQUIVOCATOR
Will she know you?

MARY
I am well known to that woman.
Time for us to meet.

You will lead her
In triumph through Paradise?
She will walk
The streets of heaven?

MARY

Or hell – the dens of hell.
That is my gift.
My torture to my cousin.
I may have been lying.
My gift is not God's –
Perhaps it is the devil's.
She will find out when awake.

Mary kisses Elizabeth and wakens her.

Good morrow, sweet coz.
I have been waiting for you.
I am here to greet you.
Welcome to the dead.

Elizabeth screams.

TWO: JAMES

The scream rebounds.
    Mary drags off Elizabeth in her coffin.
    *The Equivocator has entered the bedroom of King
James.*
    The sleeping James is woken by the scream.
    He wakes up, terrified. He sees the Equivocator.

JAMES

Who are you?

Silence.

Will you hurt me?

6

EQUIVOCATOR

Why should I hurt you, James?

JAMES

You know my name, who are you?

EQUIVOCATOR

Who do you want me to be?

JAMES

How did you get in here? Are you my guardian angel?

EQUIVOCATOR

Do you want me to be?

JAMES

Yes, I do – very much.

EQUIVOCATOR

Why are you frightened?
Have you had a bad dream?

JAMES

Please, sit beside me, angel.

The Equivocator does so and takes James's hand.

JAMES

I was dreaming of my mother.
She was burning in hell.
When I was a boy,
My bastard teachers
Drummed it into my skull –
She was damned.
I would see her,
Wearing a crown of fire.

I'd wake up screaming her name.
The tutor would hear me.
He would beat me for blasphemy.

7

EQUIVOCATOR

What was your blasphemy?

JAMES

I had said my mother's name –
The blasphemy of her name.
He would beat me for it.

EQUIVOCATOR

Poor child, where did he beat you?

JAMES

Beat my head, my legs, my arse.
Beat me in the name of Christ,
Till I shat myself once out of fear.
He did not stop –
Neither did I.
I was a sewer, a midden,
A cesspit of my own making.
When he did stop,
He broke the rod over my head.
He was crying.
It has to be thrashed out of me,
My mother's sin, he said.
I may be the young king,
God was still my master.
He served God and the kirk.
I must stand abject before Jesus.

He waited for me to rise,
To bow, thank him for his kindness.
I did not do that.

EQUIVOCATOR

What did you do, then?

JAMES

I put my hand into my shit.
I began to spread it

8

All over my body, my face, my hair.
He did not try to stop me.
He watched me as I went on and on,
Smelling of dung,
My own filth.

EQUIVOCATOR
Did he say nothing to you?

JAMES
He said, child,
You are good at heart.
You show you are grateful
For God's forgiveness.
This is how you bear
The mark of the saved.
I rose, I bowed, I gave thanks.

A boy, a friend, cleaned me up.
I smelt his clean water.
It was warm and beautiful,
Like him, my first angel.
I felt safe in his strong wings.
I vowed that day to love him.
And I vowed I'd see my tutor die.

I would summon the court,
I'd say shite on him,
Send him stinking
To his salvation.
Let them know him
By the stench of him.
Let them piss over him,
Anoint him with dung
In the name of the Lord.

EQUIVOCATOR
Did you do this to your torturer?

9

JAMES

He died suddenly.
A respectable burial.
I attended his funeral.
I may even have wept.
I did weep
When they spoke of him,
The king's dominie,
Instructor to his majesty,
Most wise and gentle.
We forget what we forgive,
Though I have not forgiven.

EQUIVOCATOR

Do you forgive?

JAMES

Yes – no.
Perhaps.

EQUIVOCATOR

Your mother in your dream –
Did she speak to you?

JAMES

To be king of England –
That's what she promised me.
Is it true, my angel?

EQUIVOCATOR

Do you want it to be?

JAMES

No. Yes.

EQUIVOCATOR

Perhaps.

JAMES

I would be rid of Scotland.

EQUIVOCATOR

Why?

JAMES

Scotland betrayed my mother
And devoured my father.
He was fed to the flames of fire,
Scorching his soul.
They let him dine with gunpowder
And left him to be found.
Who did this deed? Who was blamed?
I blame Scotland and leave it to
The smell of its dirt,
Unholy ministers
Of the soiled kirk,
Bathed in Christ's blood.
The excitable elect,
Fat with righteousness,
Licking the juices of Jehovah.
I would be rid
Of those gospel-greedy gluttons.

EQUIVOCATOR

And your dear lady wife?

JAMES

My dear lady wife?

EQUIVOCATOR

Does she too long
To be rid of Edinburgh?

JAMES

I fetched her from Denmark,
Her cold winter home.
We were stranded there –
Quite some months.
Do you know Denmark?

The Equivocator shakes his head.

Then you've not seen Copenhagen.
It makes Edinburgh
Look like – like Paradise.
It makes Stirling
Look like Paradise.
My dear lady wife,
She will be rid of Scotland.
Hide – she approaches.
Hide – she does not approve
Of my angels.

EQUIVOCATOR
She will not see me.
Only those I choose to see,
See me, James.

THREE: THE CHASTE WIFE

*The Equivocator observes James's Queen Anne arrive,
but no one sees him, except James.*
    She is attended by two Ladies-in-Waiting.
    *Two Gentlemen bear James's robes. They dress him
during this scene.*

QUEEN
Good morning, my Protestant king.

JAMES
Good morning, my Protestant queen.

QUEEN
I wish you good health, my lord.

JAMES
I wish you the same, my lady.

QUEEN

Do you wonder
Why we wake you so early?

JAMES

I was already wakened.

QUEEN

I bear you great tidings.

JAMES

Tell, my shepherdess.

QUEEN

Why your shepherdess?

JAMES

As the angels, at Bethlehem,
Did appear bearing tidings
To the shepherds, so do you –

QUEEN

That would make me an angel
Rather than a shepherd,
Would it not?
No, I am not your angel,
And never will be –
I lack –

JAMES

You lack in nothing, my queen.

QUEEN

I lack one angelic feature.

JAMES

Which is?

QUEEN

Their wings –
Their strong, protecting wings.

Is that not so?
I do know
How you need them about you.
My husband,
As my consolation,
I can give you
What no angel,
No matter how beautiful,
How beloved by the lord,
Can give.
Children – I give you children.

JAMES

For which I celebrate you.

QUEEN

That is kind.
But here am I
Talking of children
And fending off angels
When there is wonderful news
To break to you.
You've let me prattle on.
Why do you?
I believe you know –
Could an angel
Have whispered in your ear?

JAMES

Tell me – I'll tell you then.

QUEEN

Elizabeth is dead.
You are her successor.
King of England and Scotland,
All hail James.

The Ladies-in-Waiting and Gentlemen do so.
James is by now fully dressed in his robes.

JAMES

Doves of peace attend this utterance.
May I enter England, champion of her virtues.
Great spirits of the dead, my royal ancestors,
Crown me here, fill me, my blood, my brain,
With deep reverence for the task I face.

Turn my soul to mercy,
Let me hear each voice
That pleads for justice.
May pity reign in my soul,
So that hatred which divides our country
Be banished from this realm.

Let England cherish all her children.
Let my man's breast be a wise,
Be a giving father,
Healing the wounds, bitter wounds,
Of Protestant and Catholic.

I am not of that faith,
Though my mother professed it,
And the ghost of that saint,
She haunts my days and nights.
Tell that to my Catholic people.

They, too, are my dearest, my own.
Let them not fear me, and I'll not fear them.
We must not do harm to each other.
I come to them as their kind parent.
James has milk to quench their thirst.
May I have balm for their sore souls.
May I be king to each and to all.
May I be a fort of gentleness.
In all but her choice of faith,
I am my martyred mother's Protestant son.

QUEEN

Excellent, my husband.

Your words show you well prepared
For what is in store.
Who first did tell you my news?

JAMES

My mother – in a dream.

QUEEN

You have abandoned
Angelic conversation
To talk with the dead?

JAMES

Through her intercession
I can cheat death.

QUEEN

Then why fear it as you do?

JAMES

Fear it as I fear you?

QUEEN

Am I death to you?

JAMES

It takes your shape, my dear.
In our bed – devouring me –
Giving me children.

QUEEN

My ladies, hear my husband –
Playing with his wife.
Sire, you are too cruel –

JAMES

I am cruel to be kind.

QUEEN

Then I'd better fear your kindness –
It will be the death of me.

Rule well – rule wisely.
I shall be beside you,
As we have always done.
Remember, my lord,
There are witches everywhere.
They are casting papist spells –
They work the will of Satan –
Trust only those who love you holily –
Your mother, your wife.
They alone protect your manhood.
May we now walk together,
As man and his wife,
As king and his queen?

James and Queen Anne hold hands.
    *They lead the procession that will turn into a royal
progress.*

JAMES

Are my people sorry
To see me leave Scotland?

QUEEN

Grief-stricken, my husband.
They speak of nothing else.
They sing of nothing else.

JAMES

I should like to hear them sing.

FOUR: THE NEW KING

The lament, 'King James Is Goin' Awa'', is sung.

SINGERS

King James is goin' awa'
Far frae lovely Scotland,

17

King James is goin' awa'
Far frae his homeland.

Bonnie James, ye break my heart,
Ye break the heart of Scotland,
Bonnie James, will ye come back,
Heal the heart of Scotland?

Our city opens its gates
And bids farewell to Jamie,
Our eyes are sore and bursting tears,
We bid farewell to Jamie.

King James is goin' awa'
Into the pit of England,
King James is goin' awa'
Into the hell of England.

Bonnie James, they'll break your heart,
They'll break your heart in England.
Bonnie James, they'll break your balls,
You'll be limping home from England.

*The music has been changing through the song into
something rougher than a lament, but it must not get
too raucous or chaotic.*

*It grows into a folk song, and again the company
sings it.*

The lark in the morning
She whistles and she sings
Through the skies of England
To welcome her new king.

The jolly ploughboy
He throws aside his spade.
Rising with the lark
He grabs hold of his maid.

They dance till they are dying

Before the king and queen.
The realm of old England
Is the cat that's got the cream.

Lizzie, she is lying
Blazing red in hell –
The devils do the dirty
On Bessie's ding-dong-bell.

James, he comes from Scotland
To rule us like a man –
And Protestants may prosper,
It's God's appointed plan.

The lark in the morning
She whistles and she sings
Through the skies of England
To welcome her new king.

JAMES
As I do welcome you –
But what is this approaching?

*A figure dressed in the exaggerated black costume of a
Puritan, bearing a large Bible, halts the procession.*

QUEEN
It is a play, my lord.
Your subjects' play for your pleasure.

PURITAN
Your majesty, I beg a word.

JAMES
My dear, shall this Puritan be heard?

QUEEN
Speak, if you be friend or foe.

PURITAN
I am of the elect, hear my woe.

God selected me for heaven,
So I am not at home on earth.
I dine on quail, bread unleavened.
I am a Puritan by birth.
Great king, great queen, give favour –
Allow my like to worship free.
We don't know death's day nor hour.
Fear God's wrath but don't fear me.
I mean no harm, not like this dupe –
The filthy, stinking Catholic Pope.

There is a burst of music.
    A figure dressed as a Pope mock-terrifies the crowd.
    He is on short stilts, covered by his cassock. On his
head there is a large mitre.
    He is attended by two minions dressed as terrifying
dogs. The dogs can breathe fire.

POPE
I smell the blood of an Englishman,
I smell the blood of an Englishman,
I smell the blood – I smell the blood –

The Pope halts before James and Queen Anne.

Great James, great Anne, I want your souls –
My dogs break beyond my control.

The dogs breathe fire.
    The crowd screams.
    The Pope goes among them, scattering holy water.

You are saved from hell's hope.
This holy water is salvation.
Believe in Jesus, believe in the Virgin.
Abandon evil, abandon sin.
Great James, great Anne, I am the sun,
I am the moon, I am the pope.

The Pope continues to scatter holy water.

I will piss on this Protestant people.
I will chase them into the fires of hell.

James rises.
  At this the chaos quells.
  James sings.

JAMES

Gentle folk, my ain folk,
I come to you from bonnie Scotland,
I come in peace with my queen.
My friends, my foes, give me your hands.

The Puritan approaches James.

Fetch me your book, good Puritan.

The Puritan gives James his Bible.
  James sings.

I will give you a Bible,
I grant you that wish,
A Bible to banish hell
And the devil's kiss.

The Puritan kisses James's hand and bows to Anne.
  James hands him back the Bible.

Fetch me that pope and his minions.

The Pope and his dogs turn their backs on James.

My wife, tame these creatures.

QUEEN

What do you require I do?

JAMES

Lady, use your gentleness.
Win them back to our cause.

The cause of God's goodness.
Do your best, girl.

The Queen calls to the Pope and his minions.

QUEEN
Forgive us, holy father.
We are new to power.
Show yourself a loving father.
Bless this our loving bower.
Bless our happy, happy marriage.
Bless our children, daughters, sons –

James screams his interruption.

JAMES
I will not be mocked.

At the scream, the Pope falls from his stilts.
  The dogs rush to help him.

I said, fetch me the pope and his minions.

QUEEN
The boy is injured, my lord –

JAMES
Let him rise before his king,
Or leave him with his injuries.
Leave him to die if he must.
Yes, he should – he must die.
He has ruined my – ruin –

POPE
I am heartily sorry, sire.

JAMES
Your heart is sorry, is it?
What about your head?
Is it sorry?

He slaps the boy.

Your face, your two smooth cheeks,
Do you have two faces, two mouths,
One that kisses me, and another,
Another conspires against me,
So you should be sorry, very sorry.

He slaps both cheeks.

QUEEN

The boy is sorry.

JAMES

I would have him horsewhipped.
His flesh scaled from him.
Left raw red, flayed,
Bleeding at the side of my bed,
Of my roads of my kingdom –
My two kingdoms –

QUEEN

Scotland, and England.

James's voice thickens into a deep Scots accent.

JAMES

Commirwald crawdon, na man comptis the ankers
Suir swappit swanny, swyn keeper ay for swatis –

QUEEN

England – remember where we are.
My good lord, show mercy.
Will you show mercy?

JAMES

Aye.

QUEEN

Shall we fetch his minions?

JAMES
Aye.

QUEEN
Shall they bring fire?

JAMES
No – no fire.
I can extinguish fire.
The fire of Rome.
I do not fear it.
But fetch me no fire.

The minions take off their masks.
They present them to James and Queen Anne.
James touches their faces.

How beautiful the soul must be,
Unclothed, stripped of body.
I thank you for your pains.
Prosper in sun, in snow, in rain.

QUEEN
My lord is tired.
We have travelled from Scotland.
He needs sleep.
See us home to where we sleep.

JAMES
Aye, sleep.
With you, my wife.

James hands her the dog masks.
Some in the company begin to carry James and Queen
Anne out.
Others begin to construct a garden.

FIVE: THE GARDEN

The company sings.

COMPANY

There is a country fair
In pain,
A country fair
In pain.
God send the king to save it.

There is a king I do love
I love,
There is a king and his queen
I love.
There is a king, a queen, a love.

Fair country, fair in love
In pain.
Fair king, fair queen I love,
In love.
I love a king, a queen in pain.

The song continues as Henry Garnet enters.
  He is blindfolded, led about the garden by the
Equivocator.

HENRY

I see a house of hidden secrets,
A house to hide a secret truth.
Who lives here in this hidden house?
The Bible says Boaz and Ruth.

The company have constructed the garden and exit.
  A young girl, May, sings the song's last verse.
  She is a maid in the household.

MAY

Whither thou goest, I go with thee,
I go with thee, I go with thee,
There is a king I do love,
A king that I do love.

*Henry Garnet, still blindfolded, but now free of the
Equivocator, puts his hands around May's eyes.
The Equivocator stays in the garden.*

HENRY

I have found you, my little maid.

May turns to him.

MAY

I let you find me.

May begins to lead Henry about the garden.

MAY

Mr Garnet, am I really helping you?

HENRY

You do me great service.
I need to know darkness
To find my way through it.

MAY

I know where I am in this garden.
I can smell every scent.
This is one place,
When I close my eyes,
I am not afraid.

HENRY

Are you often afraid?
What makes you afraid, May?

MAY

The devil.

HENRY

Only the devil?

He stumbles.
  She stops him falling.

MAY

Sometimes I am afraid of God.

HENRY

Why?

MAY

He asks for so much.
I try to be obedient,
To be a good girl,
But it's hard.
If I don't be good,
He will harm me.
Is that wrong?
To think God is harsh?

HENRY

No – He is harsh.
Pray to Him for strength.
You must do that.
Always be a good girl.

MAY

Yes, Father –

HENRY

What have you been told, girl?
My name –

MAY

It's Mr Garnet.
I do remember.
Have you enough practising?
I need to help in the kitchen.

HENRY

Of course, dear girl.
Go back to your work.

She removes his blindfold gently.

MAY

I like being here with you.

HENRY

Come back when you finish your duties.

MAY

Our mistress is lucky –
To have you tend the garden.

HENRY

We are lucky –
To have her as our protector.
If you wish to escape her wrath,
Get back to your work.

MAY

I will, Father –

She stops.

MAY

I'm sorry – so sorry.

HENRY

Child, do you see that bed of nettles?

She nods.

HENRY

Do you wonder why I let them grow?
Why should I care for such weeds?

MAY

For soup?

HENRY

Only young nettles make soup.
These are hard old fellows.
Why do they grow here?
Will I show you why?

He places a nettle and rubs it roughly against his palm, stinging himself.

MAY

Why did you do that?

HENRY

A nettle's sting I can endure.
I can tolerate much pain.
But I do not like it.
I do not ask for it.
Each time you call me Father –
You place me in mortal danger.
You hurt me.
When you are next tempted,
Remember the nettle.
My aching pain.
Resist paining me.
Remember that, my dearest girl.

MAY

I will, Mr Garnet.

She blindfolds him again.

HENRY

Obedience. Obedient. Most obedient.

MAY

Obedient.

She leads Henry Garnet out of the garden.

EQUIVOCATOR

A gentleman and little girl,
How innocent – how lovely.
We must leave this blissful scene.
We follow the path of our lawful king
To the court – the sublime court.

*Courtiers begin to assemble, demolishing the garden,
and in their centre James and his Queen.*

SIX: THE COURT

EQUIVOCATOR

The scheming court – the laughing court
The dangerous court – the loyal court –
The court crammed with Scots –
Scots clearly on the make –
The eager court of Englishmen –
English distrusting Scots –
The holy court, the pious court –
Worshipping the Lord,
Worshipping the king,
Worshipping his queen.
The hungry court, the thirsty court,
The sporting court, the hunting court,
The wondrous women of the court,
The court that breaks the heart,
The court that laughs at heartbreak,
The honest court, the lawful court,
The thieves that fleece the rogues at court,
The rich at court, the poor at court,
The scheming court – the laughing court –
The dangerous court – the loyal court –
Who is the centre of that court?
Who knows its every working?

Who is the root of the court's power?
Magnificent minister to the king –
Robert Cecil, in all his glory,
Servant to the king and queen.
What will he make of his new masters?
What tricks shall bonnie Jamie play?

Apart from Robert Cecil, the Court disappears.
He bows to James and the Queen.
The Equivocator observes the scene.

QUEEN
We have longed to see you.

CECIL
Me – your majesty?

QUEEN
You have kept us well informed.
The king is pleased.

CECIL
I do all to serve his majesty.

QUEEN
He thanks you.

Cecil bows to the King.

JAMES
To the rois of England, I turn my visage,
I say, O lusty dochttir most benyng,
Aboif the lilly illustare of lynnage
Fro the stor ryall rysing fresche and ging
But ony spot or macull doing spring.
Cum, blowne of joy, with jemis to be cround,
For our the laif thy bewty is renowned.

Through this recitation, James has dribbled slightly.
Robert Cecil stands in shock.

QUEEN

I'm sure you've heard the rumours,
You have heard how my lord suffers –
His speech is sorely affected.
The English tongue is not –
It is not natural to him.
I have been asked to translate.

CECIL

Translate, your highness?

JAMES

Aye, do you no git it, man?

Silence.

QUEEN

My husband wonders –
Do you understand him?

JAMES

See me – see you –
I reck you're a gouk.

QUEEN

My husband finds you attentive.

James now dribbles fiercely.
   The Queen attempts to wipe his mouth.

Try to control yourself, my dear.
You have heard of my husband's afflictions.

James pulls away from her.
   He walks with an exaggerated limp.

JAMES

Git your claws from my flesh.

*James approaches Cecil, dribbling, his accent growing
ever thicker.*

What are you?
A son of Satanis,
A Turk of Tartary,
Come through the boundis of Barbary?

CECIL

I am Robert Cecil,
Your majesty's devoted servant.

JAMES

Why are you looking at me?
I'm looking at you.
Shall I tell you what I see?

CECIL

Please do, my lord.

JAMES

The lorbar lukis of thy lang lene craig,
Thy pure pynit throff, peilit and owt of piy,
Thy skolderot skin, I lwed lyk ane saffrone bag –

QUEEN

My husband compliments your skin,
He marvels at its suppleness –

JAMES

Nyse nagus, nipcaik with thy schulderis narrow –

QUEEN

You have a generous face – he praises you –

CECIL

His majesty sees me for what I am.
Hard hurcheon hirplard hippit as are harrow.
Sire, I have acquinted myself with your Scottish tongue.
I thought it best to welcome you,
Should the need for it arrive.
Should you wish to speak in secrets.

James stops the limping and dribbling.
  His voice returns to normal.

JAMES

Robert, you end the game.
I am not a maimed, dribbling fool.
You do not believe my enemies' lies.
You too see me for what I am.
We did this to amuse ourselves.
You have no time for sport.
I fear you will not love me.
Will he ever love me –
What do you think, my dear?

QUEEN

Praise him, my king.
He sees through your disguise.
He sees the true man.
Not many have done that,
My lord of contradictions.

JAMES

He may be of similar mind.

CECIL

My lord, I am your servant.

JAMES

A man of singular purpose.
To serve me alone.
I thank you for your service.
I can smell loyalty off you.
You are a useful beast.
Your only secret is yourself.
That's how you trap all others –
They will tell you everything.
My wife, look what we've found –
Our first English ally,

34

Robert Cecil, most renowned,
Most feared, most special spymaster.
From this brief meeting –
What have you learned about me?
Shall I tell you in a whisper?

James whispers.

Timor mortis conturbat me.

He speaks louder.

Translate for me, Robert.

CECIL
Fear of death disturbs me.

JAMES
Then, remove my fear of death,
Remove the threat to me.

CECIL
I have my servants too –
They are in every Catholic house –

JAMES
And do they plot against me?

CECIL
Some believe they do –

QUEEN
But you know before they do –

CECIL
I am in my queen's command.

QUEEN
For this we thank you.
My lord, shall we retire?
You must be past exhaustion –

JAMES

No, you look haggard.
The journey has wearied you.
Go to bed alone.
I would not interrupt your rest.
Go to bed alone.

He leaves her alone with Cecil.

QUEEN

Do they plot against me?

Silence.

Will they kill his family?

CECIL

All are safe, my lady.
I will see to it.
Your ladies wait for you.
Go to your rest.

She exits.
    The Equivocator appears behind Cecil.

EQUIVOCATOR

May I ask you a question?

Cecil sees the Equivocator.

I, too, serve his majesty.

CECIL

In what way?

EQUIVOCATOR

In different capacities.
Sometimes I protect him.
Sometimes I question him.
Times he tells me what I am –
What he wants me to be.

I have heard him whisper,
Timor mortis conturbat me –
Fear of death, fear of life.
May I ask you a question?

CECIL

You may – but I'll not answer.

EQUIVOCATOR

I ask what you do at court?

CECIL

I respect his majesty.

EQUIVOCATOR

I witness your devotion.
It reflects well on you.
You are a fine-looking man.

CECIL

You are the first to say so.

EQUIVOCATOR

You believe yourself ugly?

Silence.

My lord, you are kind and lovely.

CECIL

No more – it is sin –

EQUIVOCATOR

To look on your beauty?
I see what I see.

CECIL

What I see contradicts you.
The truth –

EQUIVOCATOR

What is truth?

CECIL
I am no Pontius Pilate, sir.

EQUIVOCATOR
You are the king's wise minister –
Wisest man in England, Robert Cecil –
Is the truth love?

Silence.

EQUIVOCATOR
We must all love the king –
His anointed flesh.
Kiss his sweet hand.
Touch his red lips.
We must love his anointed flesh,
We must love him as we did the queen,
Adore the man as we did the dead woman.

Silence.

Do you long for love?

CECIL
I long for my lord's love.
He does not look at me like that.
There is no love.
My body – my hateful body,
My head too large,
My eyes too sore,
My lips too red,
My flesh, my flesh,
My hateful, hated flesh.

EQUIVOCATOR
My poor, dark child, Robert.

CECIL
You would make me vain –
Vanity of vanities, I reject you.

EQUIVOCATOR

I am sorry to have offended.
I wished to see you accurately.
I wished to know how you looked.
You pride yourself on knowing everything.

He touches Cecil's face.
  Cecil cries out as if struck.

EQUIVOCATOR

Why do you fear my touch, poor child?
Do you fear all who touch, dark child?
There is truth in a touch, Robert.
This body that you hate,
Say I could dismantle it?

He touches Cecil's arms.

Limb by limb, arm by arm –

He touches Cecil's face.

This hated flesh – I can rid you of it –
In return, what do I ask for?

He embraces Cecil, stroking his hair.

Tell me what you know.
As I free you from your body
With pleasure, without pain,
Tell me everything you know.
The king loves you, loves your loyalty,
Trust in that love and in my love,
As I ease you of body's burden.

Cecil breaks free but holds the Equivocator's hand.

CECIL

There is a conspiracy –
Against our beloved sovereign.

39

EQUIVOCATOR

Who conspires to create terror?

CECIL

Catholics –
They would kill the king –
I will save him.

EQUIVOCATOR

How?

CECIL

I will hear them speaking like magpies.
I have heard how they mean to steal –
Steal his precious, silver life.
They are Catholics, all Catholics.
They speak in lying tongues.
They speak in Latin and in Greek,
In Aramaic and in Arabic,
In evil languages of the world.
I understand the talk of thieves.
They mean to thieve his life,
The Lord's Protestant servant,
Most holy high anointed,
They mean to kill God.
It is written on their speckled wings,
Loud, beating, never ending,
I can hear them speaking like magpies.
Only I can hear their secrets.
They confess to me.
I know their hearts, their hatred of my king.

EQUIVOCATOR

Who are they?

CECIL

You must tell me.

How?

CECIL

You must see the foe for me –
You must hear what they speak –
Report all back to me –
Catholics – show me who they are.
They are not what they seem.
They are hidden everywhere.
This realm is rotten with them.
They are wearing masks.
Remove them from their faces.
Catholics – show me who they are.
Tell my eyes and my ears –
My body – my blood – my brain –
They who will kill the king.
I am Robert Cecil –
You have heard me speaking.
I have said the truth.
Show me where they are, Catholics.

EQUIVOCATOR

Then come with me, my lord.

CECIL

Where do you take me?
How will you take me there?

EQUIVOCATOR

I am pure imagination
Confined by intellect
And by tricks of bone and blood.
You surely know me, I've shaken your soul.
My name is Equivocation
I am your side, I am their side.
Come, your spies may well be there.
There in the lovely garden,

Attended by loving fingers,
More used to turning pages,
The pages of the breviary,
In Catholic seminaries –
In Douai, Salamanca,
In Louvain, and in Paris,
Where rats make their nests,
The rats of Jesuits,
Well versed in spinning yarns,
In stitching lies to truth,
Best soldiers of the pope.
Come here, look and learn,
Say nothing to break the spell,
Then vanish at your word.

The Equivocator brings Cecil into the garden.
Cecil observes from a distance, disappearing when he so decides.

SEVEN: CONSCIENCE

Henry works in the garden.
He sees the Equivocator.

HENRY

Who are you?

EQUIVOCATOR

Who do you wish me to be, Father Garnet?

HENRY

I am not –

EQUIVOCATOR

You are the Jesuit, Henry Garnet.
The powerful Catholic priest.
All England knows of you.

You inspire terror.
Is that what you like?

HENRY
You mistake me –

EQUIVOCATOR
I know why you must hide.
Hide in the house of Anne Vaux –
Your friend, your rich friend.
She would save your skin
And she would lose her head –
Anne, that lovely word,
Who will walk with you in Paradise.
Now she must conceal you,
Hide you behind passageways,
Lock you in strange nooks and crannies.
That is why you prowl through darkness.
You play hide and seek with savages,
Protestants who'd scald you from this earth.

Henry continues working in the garden.

HENRY
You have the wrong man –
I am gardener in this house.

EQUIVOCATOR
May I congratulate you?
I admire your work.
You do a splendid job.
How well it all thrives.

HENRY
I have asked – who are you?

EQUIVOCATOR
A man who would believe you.

HENRY

Why should I lie?

EQUIVOCATOR

Did I say you lie?

HENRY

You said you'd believe me if –

EQUIVOCATOR

If – did I say the word if?
I have no recollection –

HENRY

Your memory plays tricks perhaps –

EQUIVOCATOR

Of what precisely I've said?
No, that would not be so.
Your business is all trickery.
Is that not so, Father Garnet?

Henry works fiercely in the garden.

HENRY

Who are you?

EQUIVOCATOR

Your conscience – don't you know my voice?
I put you in danger.
But that is fair enough.
You are hiding in this house.
That puts everyone in danger.
Mortal danger.
Your devoted friend, Anne Vaux.
Her innocent servants.
Even the young maid –
Your most beloved.
Imagine that pet –
Imagine her under torture –
She will break like a flower –

HENRY

Be gone – be gone.

EQUIVOCATOR

You cannot make me do that.
You don't know how to.
I am always with you.
I will always be.
Your servant, your friend –
Your master, your cruel master.
Everyone you touch,
They will be put to death for you.
How can you forgive
Any coming to you for confession?
How can you forgive yourself –
Doing what you do?

HENRY

I do it for my Catholic faith.

EQUIVOCATOR

You traitor, Garnet.
From your lips you admit it.
You deserve only to fail.
You have let yourself down.
Let your country down.
You have failed your faith.
You have failed your God.
They will speak of your failure
Where Christ is worshipped.
They will curse your name –
In Douai and in Salamanca,
In Louvain and in Paris –
Traitor to the King of Heaven,
Traitor to his holy Queen,
Our Beloved Virgin Mary.
You have failed your God,
You have failed your Catholic faith.

HENRY

Be gone – be gone.

EQUIVOCATOR

Finish your gardening.
Do your duty.
Here comes good comfort –
Your sweet lady.
How do you look at her?
Is it with relief?
With longing – with lust –?
Answer – answer, Mr Garnet.

HENRY

Be gone – be gone.

He is working as if possessed as the Equivocator disappears.

EIGHT: THE TRUE FRIEND

Anne Vaux enters the garden.
She hears Henry's entreaties of 'Be gone'.

ANNE

My dear, do you talk to the weeds?
Does the garden taunt you?

HENRY

Is it you?

ANNE

Is it me?

HENRY

Anne, is it you?

ANNE

Who do you think I am?

46

HENRY

I don't know.

ANNE

What troubles you, Henry?

HENRY

I was speaking to the maid,
I sent her into the kitchen,
I told her, finish your work,
Next I know I saw a strange man –

ANNE

A spy?

HENRY

Myself. My conscience.
It came to me –
The shape of another man.
He told me I desired –
I lusted after you.
I had committed sin –

ANNE

We commit no sin.
We live chastely –
Like brother and sister.
I know what the Lord demands.
I do it.
I know what men want.
It is not my flesh.
It is my money.
I've removed their paws from my pocket.
Had they not done so,
They would be sorry men.
I can face an army.
So, you are safe in my home.
None shall dare harm you.

HENRY

Safe, from all earthly powers,
I do believe you,
My strong, great Anne.
But Satan is wise,
And does not serve
Our holy king –

ANNE

The king has promised the triumph of our faith.

HENRY

We must believe the same promises,
Though we know –

ANNE

We must believe –
We must simply wait –

HENRY

Wait and pray –

ANNE

Pray till our knees bleed,
Our voice hoarsens,
Pleading to God for justice?
I tell you it is hunger –
Hunger for the word of God.
Let it be heard.
Until then, we are silent.
But I tell you this too, my dear.
I am sick of silence.

HENRY

Then we must see instead, Anne.

ANNE

What is it we should see?

HENRY

The face of God, sweet woman.

48

ANNE

How can we look at such holiness?

HENRY

With love.

ANNE

Where do we find such love?

HENRY

In courage, faith, perseverance.

ANNE

I do not possess –

HENRY

Mighty woman,
You possess each
And every quality.
We shall need to see
That divine countenance.

ANNE

What shall He reveal to us?

HENRY

The beauty of Paradise,
More blue than the peacock's tail,
More rare than the horned unicorn,
More sweet than the fragrant rose,
Speckled red and stained white,
Gracing this, your home,
This gorgeous garden.

ANNE

Where we are safe in Jesus
And His holy mother.

HENRY

Revere our Holy Mother.

ANNE

She who guides us always.

HENRY

Our Blessed Virgin Mary –

ANNE

Into Her Son's arms.

HENRY

Where we Catholics may die –

ANNE

In peace and live
In His eternal love.

HENRY

So be it.

May enters.

MAY

I beg your pardon, mistress Vaux.

ANNE

What is it, child?

MAY

There are visitors.

ANNE

Who are they?
How many?

MAY

Three gentlemen.

ANNE

Do they say who they are?
What do they want?

MAY

One says he is your cousin.
He says, tell my cousin Anne –

ANNE

Is he a fine-looking man?

MAY

He is beautiful.

ANNE

He has touched your heart.

MAY

Mistress, I – I do not –

ANNE

Greater ladies than you
Have called him beautiful.
Show him to the garden.
He is welcome.

May exits.
  *Henry has been busying himself, hiding already in
the garden.*

It is Robert Catesby.

Silence.

Why are you silent?

Silence.

You fear him.
He speaks his mind.
He'd die for our faith.

HENRY

His is a frantic faith.

ANNE

And he would kill for it.
Does he torture your conscience?
The man you saw earlier,
Could Robert be him?
Could he be your conscience?

HENRY

Catesby – that creature –
He's no man's conscience.
Not even his own.

ANNE

Have you hated him always?

HENRY

I have heard him always.
He loves his own voice
As much as he loves
The sight of his own beauty.
I do admit his attractions.
He is aware that I do.

ANNE

He has come to see you, then?

HENRY

Anne, I think you do know that.

ANNE

Don't tell me what I know
And what I do not know.
That is impertinence.

HENRY

From a man to a woman?

ANNE

From a gardener to his mistress.

HENRY

I am your humble servant.

ANNE

I shall not cease to remind you.
For as long as you live.

HENRY

As long as you allow me to live.

ANNE

Were that in my power,
It shall be forever.

HENRY

It is not in your power.
It shall not be forever.

ANNE

Don't threaten me with death.

HENRY

Only God can do that.

ANNE

Or the king.

HENRY

Long may he reign.

ANNE

God or the king?

HENRY

Both – surely.

ANNE

Indeed – both.

NINE: CONESSIONS

Catesby, Wintour and their Servant enter the garden.
    They are handsome men, magnificently attired.
    Their Servant, dressed in black, stands at some distance from them.
    The Equivocator comes back to observe this scene at an even greater distance.

ANNE
Cousin, you are welcome.
Forgive me for not being prepared.
Had I known –

CATESBY
Anne, you tease me.
Why are you not prepared?

ANNE
I cannot read your mind –

CATESBY
Did you receive my letter?

ANNE
I did not, Robert.

CATESBY
That is unfortunate –
Deeply unfortunate –

WINTOUR
We should not trust letters –

CATESBY
Indeed we should not.

WINTOUR
They fall into the wrong hands –

CATESBY

So easily –

WINTOUR

So very easily –

CATESBY

It is hard to trust anyone –

WINTOUR

With a secret –
A great secret.

CATESBY

It is why I don't trust letters –

ANNE

So you sent me no letter?

CATESBY

My brilliant Anne,
How right you are.

ANNE

Why lie to me?

CATESBY

To learn from you –

WINTOUR

Your powers of deduction –

CATESBY

Remarkable, my dear.

ANNE

Why have you called?

CATESBY

Tell me, my clever cousin.

WINTOUR

My fellow recusant –
My ally in Christ –

CATESBY

Or so I hope.
I am here to see Henry.
Is he hiding from us?
Call him, Anne.
Then you may leave us.

WINTOUR

It has been a pleasure –

ANNE

Why should I leave my own garden?
Do you dare order me –

WINTOUR

You are a devout woman –

CATESBY

A fearful woman –

WINTOUR

An intelligent woman –

CATESBY

Too intelligent –

WINTOUR

Too demanding –

CATESBY

Too decisive
With Henry Garnet –

WINTOUR

We need him –

CATESBY

More than you need him –

WINTOUR

God needs him –

CATESBY

More than we need him.
You will not approve –

WINTOUR

You will attempt to stop –

CATESBY

You will be –

WINTOUR

What you are –

CATESBY

A woman –

WINTOUR

So it is decided.

CATESBY

Go away, Anne.

HENRY

Stay.

CATESBY

We wish to confess.

WINTOUR

The sacrament of Penance.

CATESBY

She cannot hear that.

WINTOUR

She must be sent away.

HENRY

Anne – stay.

CATESBY

Then let her stay.

WINTOUR

Let her hear our confession.

HENRY

I will not listen to it.

WINTOUR

We are here to confess.

CATESBY

You are under obligation.
You must listen –

WINTOUR

We each have had a dream.

CATESBY

In it we killed the king.

HENRY

Anne, leave.

ANNE

Is that your wish?

Silence.

I have heard nothing.
Neither should my gardener.
Take care what you tell.
Your dreams may destroy us.

Anne leaves the garden.

CATESBY

Strange we should both –

WINTOUR

Share the same dream.

CATESBY

A dream to kill –

HENRY

Killing is wrong.

CATESBY

If it removes evil –

HENRY

What evil?

CATESBY

A king –

WINTOUR

His government – his family –

CATESBY

Who harm our people –
Who maim and wound them,
Bleed them dry of sustenance

WINTOUR

Punish them on pain of death
For declaring who they serve.

CATESBY

Safe in your garden, have you forgotten
Who it is they are?

WINTOUR

God's people – your people –
Your Catholic flock –
They have longed for a time –

CATESBY

Our time is coming.

WINTOUR

We make our time.

HENRY

For what?

CATESBY

Revenge.

HENRY

Revenge is wrong.

WINTOUR

All revenge?

HENRY

I have spoken.

CATESBY

And I have heard you.
How can I persuade you, priest?
What if I were no penitent
Begging for the sacrament?
What if I were a prophet
Singing in praise of my God,
The one true Catholic faith.

Catesby sings.

I saw a hillside far away,
Great multitudes of people.
The lord's dominion did hold sway.
I bathed in waters from his well.
That water washed my crimson sin,
I sang as happy as the wren.

Wintour sings.

WINTOUR

This vision my lord gave to me
To rid the earth of wrath and shame,
A burst of fire and I could see
Blaspheming and unholy names,

The evil bathed in crimson sin
And sang as happy as the wren.

Catesby and Wintour sing together.

CATESBY/WINTOUR

We sing to you in confession
What we believe the Lord desires.
Stand by us when the coward runs,
And you shall see a burst of fire.
Absolve us clean of crimson sin,
Sing with us happy as the wren.

HENRY

May the Holy Spirit,
Sweet ghost of peace,
Haunt your mad hearts.
Have I guessed your meaning?
What is this burst of fire?

Will you kill so many?
Will you kill the king,
Kill his innocent family,
The nobles of this realm,
Catholic and Protestant
Together in fiery death?
Is that what you will do?
It is the work of Satan.
It is more than mortal sin.

CATESBY

I say it is not, priest.
Why do you not agree?
You risk a terrible death
At the cruel Protestant hands
Of that ignorant Scots king.
You must hide yourself,
As we must hide our hearts,

Our noble, Catholic faith,
Our hopes, our cunning.

HENRY

It is still early in his reign –

CATESBY

He has enough time.
He shows himself no friend
To our noble, Catholic faith,
Our hopes –

HENRY

So in your cunning –

CATESBY

If we use that same cunning –
We may sport our true colours.
My beauty is marvelled at,
I dress to match that beauty.
I waste treasures on their make.
The vanity of a fool?
Look closely at myself,
At those who believe in me.
How do we know we stand as one?
Can you read my raiment?
How glorious the fabric –
I am a man of many hues.
They are vestments of mother church,
The true church of Rome,
These colours her priests would wear
To celebrate the Catholic Mass,
Outlawed in this heathen realm.
You, my dear Father Garnet,
Like all priests must conceal here
The physical splendour
Of true worship to God.
In its place I put on finery.

A subtle touch, a clever touch?
Too subtle, too clever – wait.
I can put my cleverness to other uses.
I can shed my enemies' red blood.
Will you be part of that?
Will you be of use to us?
Will you give us absolution?
Will you wear Christ's magnificent motley?
There are many of us.
Are we not, Wintour?

WINTOUR

That we are, Catesby.

CATESBY

You are of our cause?

WINTOUR

He is.

Catesby eyes the Servant.

CATESBY

All here are of our cause.

May enters the garden, carrying a small basket of food.

MAY

My lords, my mistress bids me –

WINTOUR

Do we know your mistress?

MAY

My mistress is –

WINTOUR

Pray, tell us – why take this time –

MAY

My mistress –

63

WINTOUR

I believe this girl –
You see her –
She says one word only.
Dear child, do you speak English?

MAY

I do, sir.

WINTOUR

For how long?

MAY

Since birth, sir.

WINTOUR

Now here's a pretty miracle.
You sprang from out your mother,
A healthy, happy child,
Speaking fluent English.
What was your first word?
Pray, could it be mistress?

MAY

My mistress –

WINTOUR

I wager I was right.
Mistress – mistress – mistress –

CATESBY

What did your mistress bid you do?

MAY

She will bid you eat with her, sir.
You and your friend.
She sends this food for your servant.

CATESBY

My generous cousin –
She has prepared a feast.

He turns to Henry.

CATESBY
After penance, Eucharist.
Forgiveness and food.
We do ask forgiveness –

HENRY
You cannot be forgiven.

CATESBY
But I can still be fed.
We will change your mind –
Over bread and wine.

*Catesby and Wintour each take an arm of Henry's.
    They lead him inside.
    May goes to the Servant with food.*

TEN: THE DARK MAN

MAY
This is for you, sir.

*He takes no notice of her.
    She hands him food – cheese, bread, apples.*

I hope you are hungry.

He makes no answer.

Your gentlemen are handsome.

SERVANT
I've not noticed that.

MAY
Are they kind to you?

SERVANT
What's that to a pup like you?

MAY

I beg your pardon –

SERVANT

Folk should mind their manners.

MAY

Enjoy your food.

SERVANT

I don't want it.

MAY

My mistress –

SERVANT

Eat it yourself.

MAY

I am not hungry.
We are well fed –

SERVANT

Then fill your belly.
Quit my sight.
Get into the house,
Or my boot will feel your arse.

May runs out of the garden.
  The Equivocator reveals himself to the Servant.

EQUIVOCATOR

Have I frightened you?
You frightened that child.
Do you dislike children?

The Servant does not answer.

Have we not met before?
Across the sea, was it not?
Could we have served together?

The Servant does not answer.

I know the look on your face.
It is a soldier's look.
Did we not fight for Spain
Against the demon Dutch?

The Servant does not answer.

You are a brave fellow.
I remember how fiercely –
How furious – you fought
In the name of Jesus,
In the name of His holy mother –
None would be spared,
Man, woman or child,
If you were in command.
Now, what did you know best?
The secrets of great fire,
The power of gunpowder,
It could obliterate all in its way.
What was your name again?
One of your many names?
But of one singular faith –

SERVANT
My faith is my own matter.
And I did not kill children.

EQUIVOCATOR
But you'd defend your faith,
Defend it to the death.
A good man for the cause,
A good English Catholic.
A man well versed, I'd reckon,
In matters military,
Adept with all the tools
Of the fighting trade,

67

A silent man –
Capable of slicing with his blade
The rowdy and unruly
Of bawdy soldiery,
The killing and the kissing,
The secrets of powder,
Great, loud gunpowder –

SERVANT
You called me a silent man –
In that alone you're right.
I will say no more than this –
Tell your master, the spymaster,
Robert Cecil –

EQUIVOCATOR
I serve no Robert Cecil –
I serve no master but myself –

SERVANT
And I serve only Christ
And those that serve him.
If I have sent heathens to hell
For the sake of my Lord,
I rejoice in that service.
Whatever the king knows –

EQUIVOCATOR
Whatever you know yourself –

SERVANT
I have never met you.

EQUIVOCATOR
Far away and years ago,
In the low lands of Holland –

SERVANT
Is that not a tune?

I have never sung it.
No, we have never met.
In the past nor the present.

EQUIVOCATOR
Then how did I know you?

SERVANT
If you do, what is my name?

EQUIVOCATOR
Remember, remember –
I cannot quite remember –

SERVANT
And I cannot tell you.
You know nothing of me.

EQUIVOCATOR
But I think I do.
I am sure I do.
An animal's name –
Does it not sound like –
The fox, the wily fox –
Guido, or plain Guy –
Can I put it together –?
Remember, remember
I begin to remember –
That is who you are.
I do indeed know you.
I know you will kill children.
I know you know that too.
You have done it before.
Done it in the name of God.
Their blood stains your soul.
You have killed children, Guido Fox,
And you will burn in hell for it.

My sins will be forgotten.
They were committed in God's name.
Know that, sir, as well as you know my name.

The Servant leaves the garden.

EQUIVOCATOR
Two beautiful boys plot and plan,
Not knowing what's in store.
Beauty waits to be smashed,
To be thrown like shit
Into the sewers of Protestant England.
Henry and Anne Vaux fear –
Something about this night,
What happened this night –
I know what will come to pass.
How strange to know everything.
How powerless – am I like that woman?

The Queen appears

The Queen who stands neglected,
Looking ruin in the face,
The ruin of love – her husband's love,
What will be her vengeance?
May I conspire with her majesty?

The Queen sees the Equivocator.

Dare I ask this sovereign lady,
Give me your faith?

ELEVEN: ATTENDANTS

EQUIVOCATOR
My lady, how does it please you,
This new court, the English court?

QUEEN

I wonder how life fares in Edinburgh?

EQUIVOCATOR

Do you miss the rain?

QUEEN

The cold rain of Copenhagen,
It fell on me in Edinburgh.
I took comfort from that cold,
I'd left Denmark far behind me,
And I am used to exile.

EQUIVOCATOR

I know it well too, madam.
You may have glimpsed me –
I attended your husband –

QUEEN

I do not know you, fellow –

EQUIVOCATOR

I keep myself out of sight –
I serve my lord and my lady
As and when they need me,
That is how they see me.

QUEEN

So why do I see you now?
What have you come to tell me?

EQUIVOCATOR

You are a brave lady,
You risked that voyage from Denmark –
So hard – so lonely.

QUEEN

I was not brave.
I prayed for the sea to calm.
I asked for dry land,

For the fear of death to pass.
I cried out to my father
The like of such a cry
I only once repeated.

EQUIVOCATOR

When, good queen?

QUEEN

My flesh broke for the first time –
I did deliver a child –
I cried out my mother's name –

EQUIVOCATOR

Was it not another name –
The blessed Virgin Mary?
What father did you cry to –
God – the Catholic God?

QUEEN

That is treason, sir.

EQUIVOCATOR

Is it truth, madam?
While you walk these lonely floors
Asking what you cannot ask –

QUEEN

And that I will not ask
And you should not ask me.

EQUIVOCATOR

The king has stopped loving you.

QUEEN

I could have you hanged for that.

EQUIVOCATOR

Hanged for your revenge –
Revenge for his cold heart –
Revenge for his cold kiss?

QUEEN

I will not conspire against my husband –

EQUIVOCATOR

His children – and his children's children –
Cruel to a man – cruel to a woman –
Hateful and hard rejecting you,
Playing with their toys, their favourites.
Embrace the faith you believe in –

QUEEN

I believe in what the king believes –

EQUIVOCATOR

He believes in what suits his purpose.
You are no longer his purpose.
His brood mare – you've done your job.
He discards you as you must discard your faith.
Bring this house down upon itself.

QUEEN

I am loyal as the day is long.

EQUIVOCATOR

Give me your faith.

QUEEN

And get back what in return?

James enters as the Equivocator disappears.

JAMES

You look older, my queen.
The air of England –
It does not agree with you.

QUEEN

It agrees with you, my lord.

JAMES

I thrive on it.

73

QUEEN

And it thrives on you.
The English flock about you.
You are their shepherd.

JAMES

How kind, my shepherdess.

QUEEN

No, James, I am your dog –
Who smells you in the dark.
I am your horse, James –
To be spurred and beaten onward.
I am your wife and your rat –
To be torched from your house.
I am the lice between your legs –
To be scratched and hurled aside.
I am your animal, my love,
Your most useless, loyal animal –
For you have found more strange beasts
To populate the royal zoo,
And I am not of their manly breed,
So I may never enter your heart.

JAMES

My dear, that is a sonnet –
A strange one, to be sure –
No rhyme, certainly no reason.
I congratulate your art.
The air of England sharpens your wits.
It has also hardened your heart.

QUEEN

Then you can soften it.

JAMES

Pray tell how?

QUEEN

Come to our bed.

Silence.

QUEEN

Come to our bed, James.

JAMES

I cannot.
Affairs prevent me.
Affairs of state.

QUEEN

James, I beg you –

JAMES

The Beggarmaid and the King –
A comely play.
I dislike its resolution.
A happy ending – a happy marriage.
I do not believe that is possible.

*Robert Cecil enters, attended at a distance by a great
Catholic Aristocrat and a Protestant Divine.*
*The Aristocrat carries a richly jewelled chalice.
The Divine carries a jewelled book.*

JAMES

Robert, do you believe it possible –
Marriage, a happy marriage?

CECIL

I believe in my king and queen,
I believe in their happiness.

JAMES

My trusted minister –

QUEEN

Most trusted Robert –

JAMES

You are too generous to me.

All England is too generous.
You give to me all the time.
My friend, would you give me
Anything, everything that I ask?

CECIL

What do you ask?

JAMES

Your house – would you give it?

CECIL

My house is my country.
My country is my king's.
Have what I have, majesty.

JAMES

Because you give, I'll take.

CECIL

I have more houses.
Do you wish to take them?

JAMES

What more do I want of this man?
Can you tell us, sweet wife?

QUEEN

You would ask for his love,
The loyalty of his heart.

CECIL

You have that in abundance.

JAMES

I do wish I believed you.

CECIL

Believed me?

JAMES

Do you believe him, my queen?

QUEEN

Should I have reason not to?

JAMES

I think he does tell lies.
All England tells lies.
So generous, but full of lies.
They give to me all the time,
They swear undying love,
Yet they would not mourn me dead.
They say their hearts are true
Yet I live in fear of treachery.
No, Robert Cecil, I do not believe you.

CECIL

How can I prove my love, sire?

JAMES

Tell him, sweet wife.

CECIL

Great queen, how may I win –

QUEEN

My husband's heart?

CECIL

I am at his command.

QUEEN

My husband is a hunter.
He enjoys the pursuit.
He captures his desire.
He tears it to pieces.
He smells the blood –
The blood within the veins –
Of the poor, gentle creatures
His hounds devour.
To win my husband's heart,

77

You must learn to smell blood,
To sharpen your teeth,
To rip into pleasurable pieces.
When you can do this,
And prove you can do this,
You will be your sovereign's man.
Fear his enemy – follow his prey –
You will receive my lord's attention.
Do hurt – do harm – he will love you,
In return for your ravaged heart.
You must allow him to harm you.
You must be his match –

JAMES

My match in what?
In smelling the blood
Within the veins of creatures
My hounds will devour?
How you must hate me.

QUEEN

Do you say I hate the king, Robert?

Silence.

Does he hurt me – do I hurt him?

JAMES

We do, my dear, we do.
Would you kill me if you dared?
My Robert, would you save me?

CECIL

I would, my sovereign.

JAMES

How?

CECIL

I would show you who would kill.

78

It is not your gentle lady.
And you have loyal friends in this realm.
Friends who stand beside you in courage.
I shall introduce each to you.
Listen to these men.

He points to the Aristocrat and the Divine.
  They bow to James.

Most powerful,
Most affectionate
Papist nobleman,
But loyal to yourself, my lord,
Loyal beyond all doubting.

The Aristocrat steps forward and bows.

Most learned,
Most eloquent,
Most devout,
Most eager master
Of the Protestant faith.

The Divine steps forward and bows.

JAMES
What do you require of me?
I see you come bearing gifts.
What do you demand I give back?

ARISTOCRAT
I swear true allegiance
To my master, King James.
I ask no reward,
No recognition.
I only beg you, look,
With pity, with patience,
On those of my faith,
The old faith of England,

Of your martyred mother.
We suffer for the sake of Christ,
The blessed Virgin Mary.

JAMES

Are you loyal to me –
Above all loyalties?

ARISTOCRAT

To you and to Christ, to –

JAMES

His blessed Virgin Mother.
All others of your faith,
The Catholics of England,
Are they so loyal to me?

ARISTOCRAT

Not one among the Catholics –

DIVINE

Traitors, my lord,
To a man and woman.
Their allegiance is to Rome,
To its blasphemous bishops.

JAMES

Worship of the Pope –
That is blasphemy?
Who decrees this?

DIVINE

God's book itself, the Bible.

JAMES

It does – where?
I have read the Bible,
Read it often,
Have I not, my love?

QUEEN
Your eyes have sharpened in its study.

CECIL
Your soul grown strong in its knowledge.

ARISTOCRAT
Your heart is purer for its love.

DIVINE
If you love the Bible, sire,
Undertake a great mission –

ARISTOCRAT
Let your mission, great king,
Be solace for your Catholic subjects.
Stop our suffering.

DIVINE
Give us God's book, sire, in English,
Let it speak in our sweet tongue –
Let your name be immortal.

CECIL
His majesty's name is immortal for his wisdom –

ARISTOCRAT
His forgiveness –

DIVINE
His learning –

QUEEN
His love.

DIVINE
I kneel before my king.
I vow we shall fashion
A book of such beauty –

JAMES
What would you give me in return?

Do you know what I wish,
What I require from you,
Each and every one?

Silence.

JAMES

Save me from death.
I am frightened of death.
In my cradle,
I was a king, but
I felt death near me.
Sleeping beside me.
Stealing my childhood.
A witch waiting.
A demon dreaming.
When I reached man's estate,
The crown placed
On my anointed head,
Death would whisper,
Great king of England and Scotland,
I am your conclusion.

James turns to the Aristocrat.

Can you save me from death?

ARISTOCRAT

I will pray –

JAMES

Can you save me from death,
Mighty aristocrat?

Silence.

Be gone.

The Aristocrat leaves.
  James turns to the Divine.

Can you save me from death?

DIVINE

Our fate is fixed, but –

JAMES

Can you save me from death,
Great Protestant divine?

Silence.

JAMES

Be gone.

The Divine leaves.

Can you save me from death, Anne?

QUEEN

I have given you children.

JAMES

Can you save me from death, my queen?

QUEEN

Save yourself – have courage,
My coward of a husband.
Or hide behind your spymaster.
Ask Robert Cecil your question.

She leaves.

JAMES

My servant, can you save me from death?

CECIL

I will attempt with all my life.

JAMES

Have you eyes set
On whatever is happening
That would harm me?

CECIL

I have such eyes, my king.

83

JAMES

Can you show me –

CECIL

What will happen?

JAMES

Can you save me from death?

Cecil bows in silence and leaves.
  James sees the Equivocator.

JAMES

My angel, we are alone again.

EQUIVOCATOR

I have missed your majesty.

JAMES

Are you who has been chosen –
Chosen to save my life?

EQUIVOCATOR

I will save you from death.

JAMES

How?

EQUIVOCATOR

Look – this is how –
Look, my lord.
This is the Masque of Darkness.
Darkness that will reveal all.

The torrent of water.
  Music.
  The Masque of Darkness begins.

84

TWELVE: THE MASQUE OF DARKNESS

The torrent of water.
  Strange light.
  Music.

EQUIVOCATOR

The river cradles the city,
The city's calm is now.
The river bathes the city's streets,
The streets are quiet now.
The river is the city's counsel
And it keeps its secret.
The river feels where winds blow,
Winds that bring the smell of fire.
The river feeds the dream of death,
Death puts its hand into mine.
I raise my hands, I call on death
To walk with me beside the river.
I raise my hands, I call on death
To spare my king, to spare my city.
The river dreams it is on fire,
Winds that bring the smell of fire.
The river fears the dreams of death,
I raise my hands, I call on death,
I call on his ambassadors,
Conspirators to kill my king.

The Conspirators enter.
  They are robed in red, wearing black masks.
  Wintour, masked, carries a chalice.
  Catesby, masked, carries a lit candle.
  Fawkes, masked, carries nothing.
  Others carry banners of Catholic iconography, of
Christ as unicorn and lamb, of the Virgin as rose and
tower of ivory.

Some carry symbols of Catholic theology: bread,
wine, a pilgrim's staff and shell.
The banners of Christ and Mary are raised.
The Conspirators sing/chant.

CONSPIRATORS
We raise on high our standard,
The image of our Virgin Queen –
We beg for Her sweet protection,
Let us succeed in our mission.
We raise on high our Saviour,
Image of his sweet countenance.
We beg for His strong protection,
Let us succeed in our mission.
Mary, Queen of Heaven, sweet Jesus,
Faith of our fathers and our mothers,
We beg for Your true protection,
Let us succeed in our mission.

EQUIVOCATOR
Blessed Saviour, high in Heaven,
His good mother, turn holy heads
Away from this most evil act.
They march with the armies of Satan
To kill the king, the Lord's anointed.
They walk in darkness, fearing light.

The banners are raised.

CONSPIRATORS
We do not fear divine justice
As we are pilgrims' shell and staff,
We do not fear earthly hunger,
Nourished by eternal bread.
We do not fear unending thirst,
Our drought is quenched with scarlet wine.
Most loved Lady, most revered Lord,
Accept the gifts of our stained souls

And wash them clean with bread and wine –
Your divine body, your blood divine.

EQUIVOCATOR
I pray to God, to God alone,
My Saviour, hear no idolatry,
They blaspheme with wine and bread,
They mock Your body and blood divine.
This sacrament would kill my king.
They deal in shame, their faces masked.
They walk in darkness, fearing light.
I'll write their names on magic walls.

Names are flashed electronically onto a back wall.
They come with such speed, clashing, in colours,
they should be impossible to decipher individually.
Music too intensifies.
Banners are moved into battle position.
The Conspirators now face James.

CONSPIRATORS
You affront the King of Heaven,
You make Our Blessed Lady cry.
Your faith is like an infidel's,
You will burn in brightest hell,
You will know sorrow's surest sigh,
Great king on high, basest of men,
We will bring you holiest fire,
Will purge your soul with cleansing fire,
Our gift, great king, is gunpowder,
Our song, great king, is gunpowder.

JAMES
Who will save me from this darkness?
Is there one to come to my aid?
One to hear me – one to save me?
Am I trapped in this traitors' nest
Where lions roar and wolves have bayed?

Who will hear me – who will save me?

Quiet, insistent percussion begins.
    *Wintour pours gunpowder from the chalice into
a circle, surrounding James.*
    Catesby sings.

CATESBY

Our gift, great king, is gunpowder.

*As the percussion increases, Catesby holds out the
candle to Fawkes.*
    From his robe Fawkes produces a taper.
    Fawkes lights the taper.
    *At the percussion's loudest, James snatches the taper
from Fawkes's hand.*
    He extinguishes the flare.
    The percussion ceases.
    Catesby, Wintour and Fawkes remove their masks.

JAMES

Quit my sight – you stink of blood.
You cowards, your cronies,
Your face like arses,
I'll whip them sore
With your sad cocks
Cut from your broken bodies.
I will carve your skulls open,
I will dance on your bones,
Your flesh will dung the earth.
You stink of blood – quit my sight.

Catesby, Wintour and Fawkes leave the Masque.
    *James sings from Psalm 96 of the Authorised
Version.*

Oh sing to the Lord a new song.
Sing to the Lord, all the earth.
Sing to the Lord, praise his name.

Show forth his salvation day after day.
Declare his glory among the heathen,
His wonders among all people.

*The Queen and Robert Cecil enter, masked in white.
They sing together.*

QUEEN/CECIL
I sing in praise of my good king,
I swear allegiance to him,
He does unite great nations.
My sovereign is my mighty lord,
He shall scatter his enemies,
They'll flee from him who fear him.
I sing in praise of my good king,
I swear allegiance to him.

The Conspirators remove their masks.

CONSPIRATORS
We grow jealous in your stay –
See our faces now revealed,
Show our crimes where we bleed.
We would bring you gifts of fire,
Turn your throne to funeral pyre.
Remember all, remember –
We would burn you like timber.
For our true Catholic faith
We would risk God's endless wrath.
Come away, come away,
We grow jealous of your stay.

JAMES
Children of the subtle flood,
Let earth no longer entertain you.
You have made your holy vow,
But what you vowed was water,
What you vowed was water.

You would seek to kill the king,
He knows your game, you must swing.

The flashing of names resumes on the wall.

CECIL

We know who you are.
We know where you live.
We knew before your vow.
Your steps lead you here.
What do we ask you give?
Life and limb and power.

JAMES

We knew before your vow.
Give life, limb and power.

James exits.
    *The Company sing together as all exit, excepting
Cecil and the Equivocator.*

COMPANY

For the Lord is good, his mercy endless.
Be thankful unto Him, and bless His name.
It is He who made us, and we are His.

The Equivocator sings alone.

EQUIVOCATOR

It is He who made us, and we are His.

He looks at Cecil and asks:

Are we not, Robert Cecil?

Silence.

May I read your mind?

Silence.

The guilty are dead or rounded up.
Nothing to fear from those fools.

They have faced their punishment.
The king is safe and he is sound.
But what if more are guilty?
Who else did these men tell?
Did they whisper to their women?
Did their servants overhear?
Are there evil innocent young?
Who else must be rough questioned?
Have I read your mind, Robert?

CECIL

Fetch me the dead –
And those that served them.

THIRTEEN: APPETITE

*The dead bodies of Wintour and Catesby are wheeled in
before Cecil.*
   The bodies are bloodied and near-naked.
   *The Servant, Guy Fawkes, and the maid, May, enter,
guarded.*
   May carries a platter of roughly carved meat.
   A carving knife and fork rest on the platter.
   Cecil observes the dead bodies.

CECIL

All flesh comes to this.
Silken blood, dead flesh.
And such fine fellows.
Did you think them fine?

MAY

Yes, sir.

CECIL

So you did meet them?
Where did you meet?

I cannot remember, sir.

May we assist you?

He points to Fawkes.

His Spanish masters,
They excel in remembering –
Make heretics remember –
The scream of sinew –
The break of bone –
Have you heard them, Fawkes,
And rejoiced to remember?
The fruits of Catholic torture
From the vineyards of Spain,
They are your meat and drink.
Pay now for that dainty dining.
Your friends suck on hell fire.
You will soon sup with them.
What would be your last wish?

Let the child go.

You are kind to children?
To the king's children?
They would burn with him –
That was your desire.

He points to Wintour and Catesby.

Kind to their children?
Why now pity children?
Will they save your soul from hell?

That's where these two wander now,
In their filth and foulness.
They died without confession,
Blasted to burn in hell.
Torched by their gunpowder.
It did make Heaven laugh.
They were pretty fools –
Ignorant of gunpowder.
They set their own trap.
Satan seized them in his arms.
God took his revenge.
They did not escape his wrath.
They sought to send the king to hell.
That is their destination.
They had no pity.
Do you wish to follow them, Guido?
Should I pity you?
Do you wish to confess?
Do you wish to save your soul?

SERVANT

I will confess.

CECIL

To what?

SERVANT

To what you want.
I would have done the deed –
Done it gleefully – destroyed the king.
I'll face my end like a soldier.

He grabs Catesby and Wintour's hands.

I kiss my heroes' stained hands.
They have died for Christ, and so do I.
These were men of faith and fortitude.
You see them suffering in hell –

That is the hell you create, Cecil,
The hell where you are fire everlasting.
I would not piss on you to ease your flames.
They are in Heaven, among the innocent –

CECIL

Innocent as this girl is innocent?

SERVANT

Let her go.
I met her once.
She was kind to me.

CECIL

A kind child.
May she be so to me.
I do know where you met.
I do not need your confession.
I need hers.

Cecil points to the corpse.

Remove this stench.

He looks at Fawkes.

You too are that stench.
Leave with it and them.

The guards wheel the bodies out, Fawkes going with them.

Sit.

*May does so, placing the platter of meat beside her.
Cecil takes the carving knife and fork from it.*

You like roast beef?

MAY

I do, sir.

CECIL

I would watch you.
Eating – eat beef.

MAY

I have enough to eat.

CECIL

Eat – eat more.

*He takes a slice of meat from the platter with the
fork.*
   He gives it to her.
   She shakes her head.

Eat the beef.

She takes it.

Would you prefer fish?
Do you like to dine on fowl?
Is chicken your desire?
Duck or greasy goose?
Have you ever tasted lark?

She shakes her head.
   He throws her more meat.

The French eat lark.
It tastes as it sings,
Sweet and beautiful.
The Irish eat ravens.
They suck their eyes out.
They snap on their brains.
The Spanish eat robins.
They lick their breasts clean.
They stain their teeth red.
Do you know what they eat,
These Catholic peoples,
The enemies of England?

95

They dine on birds of the air,
But their favourite is magpie,
A feast of magpies.
Have you tasted its flesh?

MAY

Magpies are unlucky, sir.

CECIL

Only when they are alone.
They tend to fly in pairs.
Sometimes you see them –
Chattering together,
In Mrs Vaux's house.
The house where you worked.
Were there many magpies –
Did you hear them speaking?

MAY

I did not notice –

CECIL

Eat – eat more beef –
Try to remember.

He throws her more meat.

MAY

I cannot, sir, eat –

CECIL

I ask you to remember –

MAY

I cannot remember.

CECIL

Eat up – or tell me this.
In that house, that garden
What did you hear?

When magpies gathered,
What did they whisper?
You must have heard them.
It's how his majesty heard.
Heard how he would die.
Do you wish him dead,
His majesty James,
King of England and Scotland?
Do you wish James to die?
Do you wish to kill the king?

He holds meat up to her mouth.

Eat.

MAY

Cannot.

CECIL

Eat.

MAY

Cannot.

She chokes on the meat.

CECIL

Eat more, girl.
Eat and eat.
Or else tell me –
What did magpies whisper?
Who heard them?
Did he hear them –
Henry Garnet?
Did he know what they planned?
Would he kill the king?
Eat.

MAY

I can eat no more.

CECIL

I know your like, poor girl.
I pity you always.
You're famished with lack of meat.
Too much is your pleasure.
You will die with beef.

MAY

I can eat no more.

CECIL

You have had your fill.

MAY

Yes, my fill.

CECIL

I do not believe you.
You are being too polite.
How refined you are.
Anne Vaux has trained you well.
Silent as a lady –
Restrained as a lady,
Restrained in body, in mind –
Well trained to lie.

MAY

I don't tell lies, sir.

CECIL

Then why be afraid to eat?
You say you tell the truth.
No one can have enough of truth.
It can harm no one.
You are absolutely safe.
Safe as houses, safe as gardens.
Mrs Vaux's garden –
Is it beautiful?

Very beautiful, sir.

Who tends it?

Mr Garnet, sir.

He tends it well –
He protects it from weeds?

He lets them grow, sir.
In moderation.
Weeds too are God's creation.
Each thing feeds –

So he'd feed all things,
He welcomes all birds,
He loves the lark and thrush,
He praises the robin,
He listens to magpies,
What did they tell him?

I do not know, sir.

Was it of blood?
Hold out your hands, your two hands.

He raises the carving knife and fork.

Did they speak of blood?
Did they sing of death?
Did he know their song?
Did he know what they spoke?

The fork goes into her hand.

Are you going to tell me?
What did he know?
What did Garnet know,
Father Henry Garnet?

The knife is now above her fingers.

Did he know about the king –
That they would kill the king?

May howls with fear.
    The knife suddenly goes to her neck, silencing her.

Far, far away, this is how they punish
Disobedient servants –
I will not cut your head off –
But your naughty fingers –
One by one – I'll slice them off.

The knife goes back to the fingers.

If this knife were to slip –
It might cut your hand off.
Then it could slip again
It would cut your arm off.
How near to your head –
How very near your handsome head –
You would be the meat then,
Meat for fat worms.
You would watch them eat your eyes,
Burning in hell,
Because you would not tell me –
Did he wish to kill the king?

MAY

Yes.

CECIL

Call it out.

MAY

Yes.

CECIL

What is yes?

MAY

He knew everything.

CECIL

Henry Garnet knew –
Father Garnet knew –

MAY

Father, forgive me.

CECIL

You have saved yourself, good girl.
Now do your work.
Clear away the mess.

He watches her work as she weeps.

MAY

God, forgive me.
Blessed Virgin, forgive me.

*Light on Henry Garnet praying in his prison cell.
May squeezes bloodied juice from the meat.
She smears herself.*

Father, forgive me.
Mistress, forgive me.

May exits with the platter, meat, fork and knife.

Cecil now faces Henry Garnet.

CECIL

We know all that you know.
Your servants have confessed.
The dogs in the street know.
The birds of the air sing it.
You will be executed.
Hung, drawn, quartered.
Your friends wait in hell.
They will welcome you.
Satan himself is delighted.
Your deeds are news in hell.

HENRY

Have you been to hell?

CECIL

Why should I go there?

HENRY

To find your reflection –
To find out what you wished –
You wished me to kill the king.

CECIL

I am his majesty's most devoted –
Most obliging – most respectful –

HENRY

Most lying – most triumphant –

CECIL

I celebrate my lord.

HENRY

He does not love you.
His lack of love is your hate.

You hate the king.

CECIL

I serve his majesty,
I serve her majesty,
She looks on me with kind eyes.

HENRY

Most lying –

CECIL

Stop your tongue –
I'll have it ripped out –

HENRY

Frighten my servants –
They'll tell you anything –
You torture children –
I will not be tortured.

CECIL

They have confessed –

HENRY

It was not confession.
You had no power –
You had no faith –

CECIL

I had power –

HENRY

It was worthless.
You had no faith.

CECIL

I believe –

HENRY

In nothing.

CECIL

I believe –

HENRY

God has deserted you.

CECIL

I am –

HENRY

In hell –
In hell –
In hell –

CECIL

I am not –

HENRY

You are in hell.

Cecil is silent.

You can be forgiven.
You can have me released.

CECIL

From where – the house of the Lord?
I know what I have done.
I did it for my king, my God.
King and God – which to choose?

Silence.

Go for the king.
I don't believe in God.
I try to believe in God.
This is what I confess to you,
One Englishman to another.
There is no God – desolation.
You say I have a soul.
I say I have a body.
That body has no joy.

HENRY

That body's lost its soul.
Robert Cecil, strange child,
I see your countenance.
What do you believe?
My Protestant son, find God.

CECIL

Where?

HENRY

Wherever you look.

CECIL

I only see my king.

HENRY

Because he will forgive?

CECIL

Because he will forget.
God does not forget.

HENRY

He has forgotten me.

CECIL

Then you should forget him.
I leave you, holy fool –
Leave you to your conscience.

Cecil fades.
The Equivocator appears.

EQUIVOCATOR

How does he know me?
Have you told him?
Have you spoken under torture?
The way the world works.
You know that at least.
So do I – your conscience.

HENRY

I last saw you in her garden,
The garden of Anne Vaux.
Now you are my jailer,
Are you to torture me?

EQUIVOCATOR

Torture you with the dead,
All those who did conspire –
They have blasted or bled
Their way to pure perdition.
And their suffering – to what end?
A list of names forgotten,
You are the last of that line,
The servant of Jesus,
Jesuit killer of the king,
Father Henry Garnet.
Could you obliterate yourself,
Tear limb by limb apart,
Eye by eye, arm by arm,
As if you did not live,
You did not exist.
What will you find in heaven?
The torture of the dead –
The torture of God,
The torture of His Son –

Henry looks at the Equivocator.

HENRY

You look like my son –
That is if I had a son.

EQUIVOCATOR

I should have had a son,
I should have had a child –
The cry of the eternal priest.
I expected better, Jesuit.

You grow old and foolish.

HENRY

I am on the point of death.

EQUIVOCATOR

Defending the faith.
As reward for that defending,
What do you want me to do?
I would bring you peace –
What would bring you peace?

HENRY

There is none to help me.

EQUIVOCATOR

There is one –
You know her.

HENRY

I cannot bring her here.

EQUIVOCATOR

She asks to be admitted.
Indeed, she does insist.
She will not be refused.

HENRY

What harm have I brought her?
What more can I do?
Even in my dreams she is not safe.
My illusions destroy her.

EQUIVOCATOR

Anne Vaux is here, Garnet.

Anne Vaux appears, dressed entirely in black.

ANNE

You think I'd be refused?

HENRY

Why are you in black?

ANNE

It is not for you – not widow's weeds.
They are for my guiltless maid.
She is dead – dead at her own hand.
The wind seemed to wash her swaying body.
Her lips were open as if they still screamed,
Begging God's forgiveness, your forgiveness.
It was not the rope took that darling's life,
Not the pull and break of that lovely neck.
Her heart exploded in bursts of fire.
They did succeed in killing a poor child,
But she was a servant girl, not a prince –
She will be forgotten as they remembered.
I will not betray her with any name.

HENRY

I add that girl's death to my list of woes.

ANNE

I do not come to torment you, my friend.

HENRY

The sight of you is comfort.
I did not hope –

ANNE

There is always hope.

HENRY

There is not much, Anne.

ANNE

This is a hard place.
Cold and silent.

HENRY

I am sick of silence.

ANNE

Then we must see instead.

HENRY

What is it we should see?

ANNE

The face of God, sweet man.
Look at it with love.
Find it in courage,
Find it in faith,
In perseverance.

HENRY

I do not possess –

ANNE

You possess each
And every quality
Needed to see
That divine countenance.

HENRY

The blue of paradise.

ANNE

Where we are safe in Jesus.

HENRY

More blue than the peacock's tail.

ANNE

And His Holy Mother.

HENRY

More rare than the horned unicorn.

ANNE

Revere our Holy Mother.

HENRY

More sweet than the fragrant rose.

ANNE

She who guides us always.

HENRY

Speckled red and stained white.

ANNE

Into her son's arms,
Where we Catholics may die
In peace and live
In his eternal love.

HENRY

So be it.

ANNE

So be it.
Wait for me in Paradise.
You have taken my life.

Anne disappears.

HENRY

She is gone.
Beloved woman.

EQUIVOCATOR

You've used her life.

HENRY

I thought it for the best.

EQUIVOCATOR

You judge yourself softly.
There is one who might not.

HENRY

You speak of the king?
Let me plead for my life.
I would have an audience –
An audience with the king.

EQUIVOCATOR

This is your vision –
That will be granted.

James appears.

JAMES

Priest, I've heard my mother.
She calls me from her grave.
See what I do to serve her.
I came to hear you confess.
Your crime is most terrible.
You'd be rid of me, wife and bairns.
You'd let them put us to the stake.
My babies' screams would rend heaven –
They suckled at my lady's breast,
They'd be torn by gunpowder,
Torn asunder by gunpowder.
Their dam would die in streams of blood,
A torrent of blood, a mountain of fire.
The men who'd do this dirty deed,
Garnet, you heard their desire,
Their murderous crime,
You absolved them of stain or sin,
I look at you and see Lucifer.
Your prayers are hymns to false gods,
You are a priest of Baal,
A prophet of Beelzebub.
May the moon and stars
Blight your black sun.
Here I myself come to pass judgement –
You tried to murder myself and my family.

HENRY

Through God's mercy you have survived.
I prayed for that mercy to succeed.
Was that prayer to Baal and false gods?
I am an ordained minister of my faith.

I am bound by seals of confession.
I cannot whisper another man's sins.
If you hear your mother in her grave,
Then hear this man on point of dying,
At the edge of his own longed-for grave.
I wished you and yours no ill or harm.
Your brood is innocent as grass is green,
As day is short and night is long.
I ask forgiveness I could not save you.
My priestly duty put me in that hell –

JAMES

And hell is now waiting to greet you.
You and all who would betray their king.
They received Eucharist from your unholy hand,
Your hands, Henry Garnet, your undone hands.
This passes all the rest – it passes all the rest.
Not men, but devils devised this –
Not men, but God – God defeated it.
The servants of the Lord, they rejoice
As I rejoice, my children rejoice.
You will go to meet God disfigured.
I show you neither mercy nor comfort.
I do to you what you would do to me.
My mother begs me, forgive the priest.
Give him softer death than the brute beasts –
Beasts that would rip my child's fragile flesh.
I say his is the greater, baser offence.
Let his death be all the slower, sorer.
You asked your conscience for my audience.
In your vision I've appeared and sentenced.
It is death, Henry Garnet, it is death.

Henry grabs James's hand.

HENRY

I am frightened of death, majesty.
Frightened of falling into hell.

Fall, and be afraid,
For you climb the gallows.

HENRY
If I look down, I will die.

JAMES
A merciful release for us both.

Henry grabs James's face in his hands.

HENRY
What am I to suffer?
The sins of the flesh.
The torture of the body,
Alive and suffering,
Dead and suffering,
Hung, drawn, quartered,
Each inch of flesh agony,
Killing a king, not killed.
You are man as much as woman,
As Catholic as you are Protestant,
As Scottish as you are English,
A being mortal and divine,
Confounding all confusion,
James, you are the future,
I am the past forgotten.
How could you not survive,
How could I not die?

He kisses James.

You have feasted on doubt,
Drunk your fill of it,
Shat its poison from you,
Pissed it into the wind.
James, cloaked in ambiguity,
Learned and learning,
Master of many truths,

I know of only one –
I believe – I believe –
I do believe that I believe.
My sovereign king, help me.
My conscience, help me.

Silence.

Help me to believe myself.

James leaves him.
   He turns to the Equivocator.

I am in agony, my conscience.
Help me – I will fall.

The Equivocator leaves him.

I will fall into hell.
I am frightened of death.

Fade.

FIFTEEN: ASSEMBLY

The Court of James assembles in its grandeur to hear a sermon. They sing a great hymn of thanksgiving and praise.

COURT
The Lord hath blessed thee by his power,
He hath brought our enemies to nought.
He gave to us the day and the hour,
He grants each favour we have sought.

Blessed art thou by most high God above,
Excel all creatures of the earth.
Thou art steeped in all abiding love,
The Lord bestows your divine worth.

The Protestant Divine delivers the sermon of thankfulness.

This day of ours,
This fifth of November,
A day of God's making,
Scripture is fulfilled.
If ever there was a deed done,
Or a day made,
By God in our days,
This day
And the deed of this day
Was it.
This day, we all know,
Was meant to be the day
Of all our deaths.
Many were appointed,
As sheep to the slaughter.
Nay, worse than so.
If it had been done,
We all had been undone.
That day was disappointed by God –
We were all saved,
That we might not die, but live
And declare the praise of the Lord,
The Lord of whose doing
That marvellous deed was –
Of whose making this joyous day
Is what we celebrate.
We have therefore done well
That this day should not die.
Let it be consecrated
To a perpetual memory
Throughout all generations.
In accomplishment of this order
We are now here in the presence of God,
His angels and his men,
Confessing this his goodness,

And ourselves eternally bound
To him for that goodness.
Our joy no man shall take from us.

*The Company shout in unison, raising their arms to
James and the Queen.*

COURT

Our joy no man shall take from us.

James turns to the Divine.

JAMES

Good priest, I bless your wisdom.
God has saved us from infidels.
They would rain baskets of blood on our heads.
Scatter our bodies over the face of the earth.
We have destroyed the bloody claw.
Yet my government, my priests, my people –
I beg you keep your vigilance.
Danger never dreamt of – that is the danger.
But if the strength of the Lord be our joy,
The very joy of the Lord be our strength.
And on this day of dear remembrance,
God loveth that our joy should be full.

There is music.
   The Court celebrates.
   *The Queen looks at James, who does not return her
look.*
   James is surrounded by young men.
   Robert Cecil comes near her.
   She smiles and he walks past her.
   James too exits.
   The Queen is alone.

EQUIVOCATOR

Woman, why are you alone?

QUEEN

I am in my lord's service.

EQUIVOCATOR

Is that what you believe?
What do you believe?
I have heard you pray.
I breathed the words before you spoke.
What words would you breathe now?
Your foolish, wise husband,
Confuse him with secrets,
Contradict, win back his heart.

QUEEN

His heart has hardened.

EQUIVOCATOR

And so has yours.
Do you wish it softened?
There is a woman you should meet.

He presents Anne Vaux, now heavily veiled.

She knows your wounded soul.

QUEEN

What does she want?

EQUIVOCATOR

She wants to give you faith.

QUEEN

What is faith?

ANNE

The belief that is passed
From generation to generation,
The blessing that is upon you,
And upon your children.
Shall generations bless you?

Great queen of England,
Do you serve the Queen of Heaven?

QUEEN

I am the handmaid of the Lord,
Be it done unto me according to thy word.

ANNE

I've heard whispers of a great secret.
Are you of our true faith?
Why have you converted?

QUEEN

The heart has its reasons.

ANNE

Are your children faithful?

QUEEN

The danger never dreamt of –
That is the danger.

EQUIVOCATOR

Give me your faith.

ANNE

Then England –

QUEEN

Will be well served by my children.

ANNE

The fuse has been lit.
There is no peace.
We must wait and watch.
Wait and pray.

The women's hands join together.

EQUIVOCATOR

Give me your faith.

THE NAMES OF THE CONSPIRATORS

Robert Catesby
Thomas Wintour
John Wright
Thomas Percy
Guy Fawkes
Robert Keyes
Thomas Bates
John Grant
Robert Wintour
Christopher Wright
Ambrose Rookwood
Everard Digby
Francis Tresham

Page 23

JAMES

Henpecked brown crow, the world thinks you worthless,
Lazy, large, fancy boy, always ready for drink.

Page 31

JAMES

To the rose of England, I turn my face.
I say, O lusty daughter, most benign
Above the lily, of beautiful lineage,
Rising royal from fresh and young stock.
Without spot or stain throughout spring,
Bloom of joy, come, crowned with gems –
Your beauty is renowned throughout your life.

Page 33

JAMES

The barren look of your lean, long neck,
Your poor shrivelled throat, plucked and well worn,
Your scorched skin the colour of a yellow bag . . .
Foolish miser, cheeseparer with thick shoulders . . .

CECIL

Hard as a hedgehog, limping, with hips like a harrow.